Build the Bridge

Letters on Shaping Culture: Where IT and Business Work as One

A. H. Robinson

Published by Harborview Publishing, LLC

ISBN: 9798349519390
First Edition

Printed in the United States of America

Contents

About the Author

Dr. A. H. Robinson is a seasoned IT leader, educator, and mentor known for his clarity, discipline, and grounded approach to leadership. With over 20 years of experience spanning higher education and enterprise technology, he's earned a reputation for guiding teams through complex challenges with focus and purpose.

From systems engineer to CIO, Dr. Robinson has led high-stakes initiatives that combine operational excellence with long-term strategic vision. His calm, thoughtful leadership has earned the trust of stakeholders in environments where precision and people both matter.

What sets Dr. Robinson apart is his belief that great leadership isn't just about what you know—it's about how you think. Through his writing, teaching, and mentoring, he helps others sharpen their thinking, communicate with integrity, and lead with intention.

Build the Bridge is his third book, following *The Disciplined Mind: How High-Performers Think Clearly, Communicate Honestly, and Lead Wisely;* and *Leading IT with Purpose: Letters on Using ITIL to Build Teams, Trust, and Tech That Works.* In this collection of real-world letters, Dr. Robinson offers practical tools and timeless principles for leaders who want to close the gap between business and technology—and do it with clarity, courage, and conviction.

About this Book

Build the Bridge isn't just a leadership book—it's a mentor in print.

Born from real-world experience and sharpened through years of helping companies transform, this book delivers a no-fluff, high-impact guide to leading in a digital-first world. Written as a series of personal letters from mentor to mentee, each chapter cuts through the noise and gets to the heart of what modern leadership demands.

Whether you're a CEO, CIO, or other executive, team leader, or rising talent, you'll learn how to:

- Align your business and IT teams around outcomes that matter
- Lead confidently, even when you're not technical
- Build a culture where digital tools become business accelerators
- Make smarter tech decisions without getting lost in the weeds
- Turn transformation into momentum—not burnout

This isn't theory. It's what works. Shared with candor, clarity, and the urgency of someone who's been in the room, made the calls, and knows what's at stake.

If you're ready to lead change with purpose—and finally bridge the gap between vision and execution—this book is your starting point.

Introduction

Dear Leader,

There has never been a more critical time to lead with clarity, purpose, and technical savvy. Technology is no longer a side conversation or a department buried in the basement. It is the thread that runs through every customer experience, every operational shift, and every innovation. Yet, too often, IT leaders are either left out of strategic conversations—or they enter the room speaking a different language.

This book is for those ready to change that.

Whether you are an experienced CIO or a business leader trying to make sense of digital transformation, *Building the Bridge* is your playbook. It does not offer silver bullets. It offers clarity. It does not lecture. It invites. Through a series of candid letters, this book guides you through the mindsets, mechanics, and muscles needed to lead IT—and your organization—with intention.

A Letter, Not a Lecture

Each chapter is written as a letter—not a whitepaper, not a theory dump, but a conversation. That format is intentional. The best leadership lessons are shared, not shouted. They come from lived experience, not slideshows. These letters draw on real work, real challenges, and real wins from over two decades of leading IT in complex, high-stakes environments.

You will not find hype here. What you will find is grounded guidance—on navigating the politics of digital alignment, translating technical wins into business value, leading through change without the fluff, and building a digital culture that sticks. Each letter ends with two reflection questions. You will also find tools for action, additional reflection questions, and exercises at the end of the book because insight without action is just noise.

For Leaders Who Want to Lead

This book is not just for people with "IT" in their title. It's for leaders who understand that digital leadership is, in fact, business leadership. If you are trying to:

- Earn a seat at the strategy table (and keep it)
- Align technology with what matters to the business
- Communicate across functions, not just within your silo
- Build resilient, future-ready teams

- Or, simply lead with more clarity, intention, and impact

Then this book is for you.

It's also for the people who are tired of the buzzwords. Who wants less spin and more substance. Who care less about being called "innovative" and more about being effective.

Why Letters?

Letters create space for reflection. They slow the scroll. In a world that glorifies urgency, letters invite thought. They offer perspective. Each one is designed to feel like a mentor's note or a trusted colleague's nudge—a space to think, not just react.

You'll find letters on everything from IT and business strategy to collaboration, as well as digital culture and leadership presence. Some will challenge you. Others will validate what you already know. All are written with respect for your experience—and belief in your growth.

Why Now?

Digital transformation is no longer a project. It's a posture. And the most effective leaders are not just adopting new tools—they're building new muscles. The ability to lead with clarity, translate complexity, and navigate change with intention is what sets apart those who thrive from those who stall.

This book gives you the tools to do just that.

How to Use This Book

Begin at the beginning or skip to the letter that addresses your current challenge. Use the tools. Reflect on the exercises. Share them with your team. Each stands alone, but they build on one another in momentum and message. Together, they create a leadership path that's as practical as it is powerful.

This is not just a book to read. It's a book to use.

Let's get to work.

.With purpose,

A Fellow Leader

Letter 1: On the Role of IT in Modern Business

Dear Leader,

There's something you need to understand right out of the gate: IT isn't just part of your business—it is your business. I don't say that for shock value. I say it because every high-growth, high-impact, high-resilience organization I've worked with has figured this out.

I've been in tech for over three decades. I remember when IT was that quiet department in the basement. People only noticed us when something broke. No one invited IT to the strategy table. We weren't expected to shape growth, customer experience, or innovation. We were expected to keep the lights on.

But things changed. Fast.

Digital transformation, cloud computing, big data, AI, cybersecurity—it all exploded.

And suddenly, companies realized they couldn't scale, compete, or survive without a real IT strategy. That's where you come in. The most successful leaders I've worked with see IT not as a function, but as a capability. They don't just fund it. They shape it. They align it with outcomes. They drive it from the top.

So, let's unpack what this looks like in practice. Starting with a word you'll hear a lot from me: alignment.

Strategic Alignment: The Core Equation

Let's define it. Strategic alignment means your tech strategy supports your business strategy—intentionally, directly, and visibly.

It means that the systems you build and the data you track help you grow faster, serve customers better, and operate more efficiently. It means IT isn't just fixing what breaks—it's building what moves you forward.

When alignment is strong, every tech investment points toward a clear business outcome. When it's weak, you get waste, friction, and missed opportunities.

The key here? Communication. Regular, structured conversations between IT leaders and business leaders.

Shared language. Shared goals. Shared wins. That's how you build trust, get clarity, and stay in sync.

The Competitive Advantage You Can't Afford to Ignore

Let's talk strategy.

Competitive advantage comes down to one thing: delivering more value than your competitors in a way they can't easily replicate. That might mean faster service, more brilliant insights, lower costs, or a better customer experience. IT plays a role in all of it.

Here's how tech drives that edge:

- **Operational efficiency:** Cloud platforms, automation tools, and modern ERPs eliminate bottlenecks and free up your team to focus on impact. Think Amazon's fulfillment centers are powered by AI-driven robotics.
- **Customer obsession:** With the correct data, you can personalize experiences at scale. Look at Starbucks and its loyalty program. It's not just about coffee. It's about intelligent offers, mobile payments, and anticipating preferences.
- **Innovation loops:** AI, IoT, and blockchain aren't buzzwords. They're the engines behind entirely new

business models. Tesla didn't just build cars—they built data platforms on wheels.

- **Agility:** The cloud lets you test, pivot, and deploy with speed. The companies that thrived during COVID weren't lucky. They were cloud-ready.
- **Insight:** Business intelligence tools give your leadership team a clearer view of reality. You can spot risks early, see trends faster, and act with conviction.

When your IT strategy is built for scale and speed, you transition from a reactive to a proactive approach, shifting from fixing problems to identifying opportunities.

How IT Fuels Every Corner of Your Business

Let's break it down.

- **Finance:** Automated reporting, predictive forecasting, and real-time dashboards transform how you manage capital and risk.
- **HR:** Recruitment platforms, performance tools, and LMS systems create a more engaged, data-driven, and agile workforce.
- **Supply Chain:** Sensors, logistics platforms, and analytics optimize delivery, reduce waste, and prevent disruptions.

- **Marketing and Sales:** CRM systems give you complete visibility into the customer journey. Data analytics lets you launch more innovative campaigns and shorten the path to conversion.
- **Product Development:** Agile tools and digital twins help you iterate faster and build with customer feedback in mind.

Every function becomes sharper with the right tech foundation. And when those systems talk to each other, you get synergy. Momentum. Velocity.

Trends You Can't Ignore

There are a few shifts that every leader—regardless of background—needs to understand:

- **Artificial Intelligence & Machine Learning:** This isn't sci-fi. AI is shaping hiring, marketing, logistics, and customer service in real time. It's not replacing leaders. It's elevating them.
- **Cloud & Edge Computing:** These models scale with your business. They cut costs, increase speed, and give your teams access to tools from anywhere.
- **Cybersecurity:** Threats aren't just IT's problem. A breach is a business risk, a brand risk, and a board-level issue.

- **Sustainability & Green IT:** Customers and investors care how you use energy, manage waste, and measure impact. Tech can help you lead—not lag—on this front.
- **Hybrid Work & Digital Collaboration:** The tools we use to connect are now the backbone of culture, innovation, and execution. They're not just communication tools. They're trust tools.

These aren't tech trends. They're business imperatives.

What I Want You to Remember

This isn't about turning you into a tech expert. It's about giving you the strategic lens to lead with clarity, confidence, and alignment.

Start asking:

- How does our IT roadmap align with our growth plan?
- Where are the silos between IT and other functions—and how do we break them?
- Are we using technology to create new value, or keep up?
- What metrics tell us whether our tech investments are paying off?

Make these questions a habit. Use them in executive meetings, planning sessions, and board updates. They'll elevate your conversations—and your results.

You don't need to know how every tool works. However, you do need to understand what it's for, what it enables, and what it costs you not to use it effectively. You're not here to manage tech. You're here to lead through it. And if you keep that mindset, you won't just survive disruption—you'll define what comes next.

With purpose,

A Fellow Leader

Reflection Questions

1. How well does your IT vision align with your business strategy?
2. What challenges might arise in executing your IT initiatives, and how can you address them?

Letter 2: On Bridging the Gap Between IT and Business

Dear Leader,

You've probably felt it already—that tension between IT and the rest of the business. It shows up in missed deadlines, tech projects that stall out, or teams that can't quite connect. I've seen it in boardrooms and break rooms alike. And I can tell you this: that disconnect isn't just annoying. It's expensive.

Misalignment between IT and business strategy is one of the most common, costly, and fixable challenges organizations face today. So let's talk about why it happens—and how you, as a leader, can fix it.

Where the Disconnect Comes From

It's not about bad intentions. It's about different vantage points.

Business leaders focus on markets, revenue, and outcomes. They want speed, clarity, and growth. IT leaders focus on systems, security, and scale. They're wired to think in terms of infrastructure and risk mitigation.

Without translation, these priorities clash. Business wants results now. IT wants to future-proof. Business sees cost. IT sees investment. Without trust and shared goals, projects derail, teams dig in, and progress stalls.

But here's the thing—when these teams align, the results are game-changing.

What True Synergy Looks Like

I've seen companies transform simply by bridging the gap between their tech and business units. Here's what happens when synergy kicks in:

- **Innovation speeds up.** With clear communication and shared goals, you don't just build faster—you make smarter.
- **Resources stretch further.** IT initiatives are better scoped and more relevant, resulting in reduced waste and rework.
- **Customer experiences improve.** When IT and business co-create solutions and value, the result is more intuitive, more useful, and more personal.
- **Decisions get sharper.** With shared access to data and context, leaders make faster, more informed decisions.

You stop building in isolation. You start building momentum.

What Gets in the Way

There are a few usual suspects I see over and over:

- **Different languages.** IT talks tech. Business talks strategy. No one translates.
- **Misaligned timelines.** Business needs speed. IT prioritizes stability.
- **Siloed planning.** IT finds out about key goals too late—or vice versa.
- **Lack of shared success metrics.** What counts as a win for one side may not have a significant impact on the other.

These are solvable. But they require intentionality. That's where you come in.

Your Role as a Connector

You don't need to know every system, acronym, or protocol. What you do need is the ability to unite people. To build common ground. To ask the right questions and create space for shared wins.

Start with these moves:

- **Create shared goals.** Bring IT leaders into strategy discussions early. Define outcomes together. Let both sides shape the solution.
- **Assign IT-business liaisons.** These hybrid roles—part strategist, part translator—keep projects aligned and people in sync.
- **Invest in cross-training.** Equip business leaders with a baseline level of tech fluency. Help IT understand market and customer drivers. Build mutual respect.
- **Implement Agile thinking.** Not just in development, but across how you work—frequent feedback, small iterations, visible progress.
- **Use collaboration tools intentionally.** Slack, Teams, and shared dashboards aren't just for communication. They're for transparency and accountability.
- **Celebrate joint wins.** When a tech initiative moves the needle, spotlight the team, not just IT, not just business. Everyone.

Case Studies to Steal From

A few stories I love to reference:

- **Netflix**: They don't just recommend shows. Their tech team sits at the table with content strategy, using viewer data to greenlight originals. That's IT shaping the product.
- **P&G**: Their IT and logistics teams co-designed a global supply chain model using real-time data. They reduced waste and increased delivery speed, not solely because of technology, but because of a shared vision.
- **Walmart**: Their data teams work hand-in-hand with operations to forecast demand, optimize inventory, and tailor pricing. That's how you use IT as a competitive weapon.

Metrics That Matter

Want to know if your IT-business alignment is working? Track more than uptime and ticket resolution.

Start asking:

- Are we co-owning KPIs that tie back to business outcomes?
- Are project timelines getting shorter, not longer?

- Are IT solutions getting adopted faster and used more widely?
- Are we seeing measurable improvements in customer satisfaction or employee productivity?

The best metric? You'll feel the shift. You'll see less friction, more momentum. Fewer debates, more progress.

What I Want You to Remember

You don't have to be the tech expert. But you do have to be the bridge.

You have to create a culture where IT and business don't just coexist—they engage in *value co-creation,* where tech is not just a cost center but a strategy partner, where everyone sees the value because everyone contributed to its creation.

The truth is, most companies don't suffer from a lack of technology. They suffer from a lack of translation. That's your opportunity.

Be the leader who connects the dots. Be the one who asks better questions. Be the reason IT and business finally pull in the same direction.

That's how you build trust, alignment, and impact. That's how you lead.

With purpose,

A Fellow Leader

Reflection Questions

1. What are your organization's primary barriers in aligning IT with business objectives? How can these barriers be addressed to foster better collaboration and understanding?
2. Can you identify areas within your organization where IT and business synergy have led to tangible benefits such as improved efficiency or innovation? How could these successes be replicated or expanded?
3. What steps has your organization taken to integrate IT into its strategic planning processes? Are there opportunities to enhance this integration to achieve greater alignment and impact?

Letter 3: On IT Fundamentals for Business Leaders

Dear Leader,

Let's level with each other. You don't need to be a technologist. But, you do need to understand enough about technology to lead with it, not around it.

I've seen far too many smart, capable leaders lose influence at the decision-making table because they avoided the conversation about technology. They'd freeze up when someone mentioned cloud architecture or predictive analytics. They'd defer to IT or vendors, hoping the strategy would sort itself out.

But here's the problem: if you can't speak the language of technology, you can't shape the vision. You can't question bad investments, guide innovation, or ensure your teams are building solutions that move the business forward.

This letter is about giving you that foundational fluency. Not so you can build systems, but so you can lead the people who do.

Why IT Literacy Matters More Than Ever

Business success today is inseparable from IT literacy. Whether you're launching a new product, entering a new market, or tightening operations, you're leaning on tech to do it.

Understanding IT means you can:

Push back when a tech vendor oversells features you don't need.

Spot gaps between what your business needs and what your systems deliver.

Ask sharper questions in board meetings and budget reviews.

Lead transformation, not just approve it.

As I mentioned in previous letters, technology isn't a department. It's embedded in everything: customer service, logistics, finance, HR, product design, marketing, compliance. If you want to lead cross-functionally, you need to understand how technology ties it all together.

Key Concepts Every Leader Should Know

You don't need to go back to school. But there are a handful of concepts that, once you understand them, will shift how you lead:

Networks & Connectivity: These are the veins of your organization. LAN, WAN, VPN—what matters is knowing how your teams connect, how your data flows, and where bottlenecks or vulnerabilities might exist.

Data Management: You're sitting on a mountain of data—financials, customer behavior, operational metrics. Good leaders know how it's stored, how it's structured (think databases and data warehouses), and how to extract value from it.

Cloud Computing: This is not just IT outsourcing. The cloud changes your cost structure, scalability, and the speed at which your teams can build and test. Know the difference between IaaS, PaaS, and SaaS—not to explain them, but to decide when and why to use them.

Cybersecurity: This isn't IT's problem. It's your liability. Understand how data is protected, what risks you're exposed to, and what your protocols are for breaches—leaders who treat cybersecurity as an afterthought pay dearly.

Business Applications: CRM, ERP, HRIS—these aren't just acronyms. They're your digital nervous system. Know what systems power your business, what they integrate with, and how well your teams use them.

Digital Literacy: This is about your mindset. Do you embrace new tools, ask data-driven questions, and push for digital inclusion across your org? If not, your teams won't either.

These concepts don't require technical expertise. They make you capable. Capable of seeing the whole picture. Capable of pushing strategy forward.

How to Build IT Literacy in Your Team

You don't have to do this alone. IT literacy should be a shared leadership priority, not just a responsibility for the CIO.

Here's how to create that culture:

Run executive workshops. Host sessions where IT breaks down key concepts in business terms. Keep them strategic. Make it safe to ask questions.

Promote shared language. Use cross-functional playbooks that define terms, systems, and priorities. The goal is not uniformity—it's clarity.

Create IT-business partnerships. Assign IT leads to central business units. Please encourage them to attend planning meetings. Let them build relationships and context.

Encourage shadowing. Have business leaders spend time with IT teams—and vice versa. You can't understand what you've never seen.

Stay curious. Read tech news. Attend cross-industry conferences. Listen to your engineers. Ask why something works the way it does.

Your goal isn't to become an expert. Your goal is never to be sidelined.

Practical Questions to Keep Asking

Here are a few questions I've used with leadership teams to keep the focus on strategy and simplicity:

Are we collecting the correct data to make good decisions?

Which systems are helping us scale—and which ones are slowing us down?

Are our teams using our tools entirely, or are we leaving value on the table?

How secure is our customer and financial data?

What IT investments moved the needle this year?

Use these in your team reviews, vendor meetings, and strategy sessions. They'll anchor the conversation in what matters most: value, risk, alignment, and growth.

The Mindset Shift That Changes Everything

The moment you stop seeing IT as someone else's job—and start seeing it as a lever you control—you change the game.

You will:

- Stop deferring tough tech conversations.
- Start setting a vision that your teams can build around.
- Inspire better questions, faster decisions, and more creative solutions.

Remember, leadership isn't about knowing everything. It's about knowing enough to make significant decisions—and creating the culture where others can thrive.

You've got smart people. Now give them a visionary leader.

With purpose,

A Fellow Leader

Reflection Questions

1. How well do I understand the core IT concepts crucial for my organization's success, such as networks, data management, cloud computing, and cybersecurity?
2. How can IT tools and systems improve the efficiency and effectiveness of my organization's operations?

Letter 4: On Building the Right Tech Culture

Dear Leader,

Let's talk about something that rarely makes it onto the strategy slide deck, but quietly determines the success—or failure—of every transformation you'll lead: culture.

More specifically, tech culture.

Now, I don't mean beanbags, Slack channels, or hackathons. I mean the mindset your organization brings to how it uses, values, and integrates technology. I mean the shared beliefs and behaviors that shape how teams interact with IT, how they approach innovation, and how they respond to change.

If strategy is what you want to do, culture is how you actually do it.

The best strategy in the world will stall if your culture isn't ready to support it. And nowhere is that more true than when it comes to technology.

Why Culture Eats Tech for Breakfast

You've heard the phrase, "Culture eats strategy for breakfast." Here's the 2025 remix: Culture eats technology for breakfast, lunch, and dinner.

I've seen companies invest millions in top-tier platforms—only to watch adoption tank because employees didn't trust the system, didn't understand it, or weren't included in its design. I've seen brilliant IT teams create elegant solutions that no one used because they were delivered without business input, buy-in, or training.

It's not the tech that fails. It's the environment around it.

Tech culture isn't about having the most advanced tools. It's about having the most aligned people. People who are empowered, engaged, and equipped to use technology to do better work.

Signs of a Strong Tech Culture

When tech culture is strong, you'll feel it. You'll see:

- **Shared ownership:** Tech decisions aren't just made in IT. Business teams feel responsible for the outcomes, too.

- **Curiosity over resistance:** New systems are met with questions and interest, not fear or eye rolls.
- **Collaboration, not turf wars:** IT and business teams co-create solutions instead of fighting for control.
- **Speed and agility:** Ideas get tested quickly. Feedback loops are short. People adapt.
- **Trust in data:** Leaders use real insights, not gut instinct, to make decisions—and they trust the numbers because they helped build the systems.
- **A growth mindset:** Failure isn't fatal. It's feedback. Teams experiment, iterate, and learn fast.

In short, tech culture is what turns a company from digital-aware to digital-powered.

What Gets in the Way

Even the smartest organizations can struggle with tech culture. Here's what typically blocks progress:

- **Fear of change:** New tools threaten comfort zones. Without clear "why," resistance sets in.
- **Top-down rollouts:** Decisions made without input from users almost always backfire.

- **Over-complexity:** Systems get too dense, too jargon-filled, too detached from daily work.
- **Lack of enablement:** If people aren't trained, supported, and encouraged to use new tools, they won't.
- **Blame over partnership:** When something breaks, people point fingers instead of fixing it fast.

Culture is fragile. But it's also moldable—if you're willing to lead it intentionally.

How to Shape the Culture You Want

You don't need a reorg or a massive change initiative to shift your tech culture. You just need to lead differently.

Here's how:

1. Model the Mindset

If you want people to embrace digital tools, use them. If you want teams to act on data, ask for it. When you lean into change, others will follow. Culture starts with what leaders tolerate, but it grows from what leaders demonstrate.

2. Invite Business to the Table

Include business teams in system design, rollout planning, and vendor selection. Ask what they need—not what IT wants to build. When people feel heard, they show up differently.

3. Make IT Human

Move beyond ticketing systems and faceless rollouts. Introduce your IT leaders. Celebrate their wins. Encourage sharing stories about how tech has helped real people do their jobs more effectively. You'll build empathy and bridge gaps.

4. Reward Collaboration

Too often, tech wins get credited to a single department. Flip that script. Recognize cross-functional success. Shine a light on teams that solved problems together.

5. Simplify the Stack

More tools don't mean a better culture. Reduce friction. Streamline platforms. Remove the tech debt that clogs momentum and frustrates users.

6. Build Champions

Find early adopters, super-users, and tech advocates inside your org. Give them visibility. Let them coach others. Peer-led change consistently outperforms top-down mandates.

7. Prioritize Enablement

Training isn't a one-time event. Build learning into the way you operate. Make it ongoing, contextual, and easy to access. And don't stop at how to use the tool—teach why it matters.

8. Connect Culture to Business Value

Track adoption metrics. Survey sentiment. Tie it to KPIs. When people see culture as a performance lever, not just an HR initiative, it sticks.

Culture as a Competitive Advantage

When tech culture is strong, transformation stops feeling like an initiative and starts becoming the norm. You build muscle memory. You increase resilience. You move faster and more in sync.

That's a competitive advantage few companies can replicate.

Take a look at companies known for innovation. Amazon. Spotify. Shopify. What they share isn't just talent or tools—it's a cultural operating system. One that values speed, feedback, and experimentation. One where IT and business are one team.

That doesn't happen by accident. It happens when leaders choose it.

What I Want You to Remember

Your culture is already shaping your tech future—whether you realize it or not.

You can let it happen by default. Or you can design it with intent.

When you lead with curiosity, include your teams, and connect tech to purpose, you create a culture that can handle any disruption.

Ultimately, it's not the tools that drive transformation.

It's the people who know how to use them.

With purpose,

A Fellow Leader

Reflection Questions

1. Where in your organization is tech culture supporting innovation, and where is it holding it back?
2. What's one small behavior you could model this week to make tech feel more collaborative and human for your team?

Letter 5: On Leading Digital Transformation Without Losing Your Team

Dear Leader,

I think you would agree that digital transformation sounds great until you're the one responsible for delivering it.

On paper, it's exciting—AI, automation, the cloud, big data—the promise of speed, insight, and scale. But in practice, it often feels like pushing a boulder uphill while juggling a reorg, shrinking budgets, and teams that are already running at full tilt.

Let me say this upfront: transformation is never just about technology. It's about people. It's about getting your teams to move forward together, through uncertainty, resistance, and sometimes outright fear.

If you want your transformation to stick, you need to lead it like a movement, not a mandate.

Why Most Digital Initiatives Stall

You know the drill. New platforms get rolled out. Consultants are hired. A glossy deck outlines the roadmap. But six months later, momentum fades. Adoption is patchy. And your people are quietly wondering, "What's changing here?"

Here's why that happens:

- **Lack of clarity:** People don't understand why it matters—or how it affects them.
- **Poor communication:** The plan was shared, but not explained. No two-way dialogue.
- **Overload:** You introduced new tools, but nothing was taken off their plate.
- **Fear of failure:** Teams are afraid of looking slow, behind, or replaceable.
- **No visible wins:** Without quick wins, the whole thing feels abstract.

Fixing this doesn't require more tech. It needs better leadership.

The Four Phases of Leading Change

Digital transformation isn't a one-time event; it's a series of shifts. I like to break it down into four key phases:

1. Inspire Belief

Start with the story, not the systems. Paint a clear picture of the future. Why are you changing? What's broken? What becomes possible on the other side? Connect the dots to real customer problems and real business pain. If your team doesn't believe, they won't move.

2. Equip the Front Line

You can't transform from a boardroom. Your managers, team leads, and frontline employees need tools, training, and clear expectations. Ensure that every layer of the organization knows its role and feels supported in delivering it.

3. Remove Barriers

Look for friction. Where are systems clunky? Where's the data siloed? Where are the policies outdated? Remove what slows people down, and watch adoption skyrocket.

4. Celebrate Progress

Transformation can be exhausting. Build in feedback loops. Spotlight success. Share stories of real teams doing real work differently. Let people see themselves in the change.

When you lead across all four phases, you create momentum that builds instead of burns out.

The Role of Trust in Transformation

Trust is the currency of change. Without it, you're just announcing things. With it, you're enrolling people.

Here's how to build trust in the middle of disruption:

- **Be transparent:** If something's hard, say so. If you don't have all the answers, say that too.
- **Ask, don't assume:** Involve your teams early. Let them shape the solution. You'll get better ideas—and deeper buy-in.
- **Follow through:** Don't overpromise and under-deliver. Make fewer commitments, but keep every one.

People don't need perfection. They need presence. They need to see that you're listening, learning, and adjusting.

Your Job Isn't to Know Everything

One of the biggest traps leaders fall into during transformation is the misconception that they must be the expert. You don't.

Your job isn't to have all the answers. It's to:

- Create space for smart people to solve complex problems
- Set clear priorities and guardrails
- Keep the team aligned and energized

In other words, lead the system, not just the strategy.

What I've Learned from the Trenches

Over the years, I've helped companies of all sizes navigate significant transformation efforts. Here's what I've seen work:

- **Co-create solutions:** The best digital tools are built with input from users, not just handed down by leadership.
- **Pilot fast, scale later:** Test in small pockets. Refine. Then go wide.
- **Name your champions:** Find the believers, the early adopters, the natural communicators.

- **Balance pace and patience:** Move fast enough to show progress, but slow enough to bring people with you.

There's no perfect formula. But if you prioritize people and stay close to the ground, you'll make better bets and fewer missteps.

What I Want You to Remember

Digital transformation isn't a tech project. It's a leadership practice.

It's the practice of listening, adjusting, unblocking, and inspiring. Of helping people move through fear and into ownership. Of connecting strategy to action, day by day, decision by decision.

Again, you don't need to be an expert. You need to be the one who never stops asking: How do we make this real?

Lead like that, and your team won't just survive transformation; they will thrive. They'll own it.

With purpose,

A Fellow Leader

Reflection Questions

1. What barriers—technical or emotional—are slowing your team's transformation today?
2. How are you helping your people feel ownership instead of overwhelm during change?

Letter 6: On Leading with Governance and Compliance

Dear Leader,

Here's a truth you've probably lived: technology isn't just a tool—it's a force. It powers how we scale, how we serve, and how we stay relevant. But with that force comes a kind of responsibility many leaders tiptoe around: governance and compliance.

Too often, these words feel like bureaucracy. Like brakes. Like the stuff that slows down progress. But when done right, governance and compliance aren't just safeguards. They're accelerators. They give your teams clarity. They build trust. They create the conditions where innovation can actually thrive without burning the house down.

So let's reframe how we think about them. Let's talk about how governance and compliance aren't about saying no—they're about creating the guardrails that let you say yes more often and with more confidence.

Governance: More Than a Checklist

Think of IT governance as your organization's decision-making backbone. It's how you make sure the technology you're betting on actually supports the business you're building.

Frameworks like **COBIT** aren't just academic—they're practical blueprints. They help you:

- Align IT goals with business strategy
- Define who decides what—and why
- Track performance and accountability

It's about structure. It's about visibility. But most of all, it's about consistency. When governance is strong, your teams know how decisions get made. They know what's expected. And they know how to course-correct without waiting for a crisis.

Want to see it in action? Picture a company using COBIT to vet every major tech investment. Instead of reacting to the loudest voice or latest trend, they use a scorecard. Strategic fit. Risk exposure. ROI. Adoption readiness. That kind of clarity doesn't slow you down—it helps you move faster with fewer regrets.

ITIL and ISO: Making Governance Real

COBIT sets the direction. But what makes it work is when it's paired with frameworks like **ITIL** and **ISO/IEC 27001**. ITIL helps you design services that match business needs—while staying flexible. ISO gives you the structure to manage information security with rigor.

Together, these frameworks move governance out of theory and into workflow. For example, defining SLAs during the ITIL Service Design stage forces alignment before a project ever begins. ISO's emphasis on continual improvement means you're not just compliant today—you're resilient tomorrow.

Metrics That Matter

Governance isn't just about process—it's about progress. And that means metrics.

Track things like:

- Project success rates
- Risk mitigation effectiveness
- SLA compliance
- System uptime

But don't just measure. Review. Reflect. Adjust. Use frameworks like **NIST's Cybersecurity Framework** to build detection and response into your governance DNA. The overlap between NIST and COBIT is powerful—NIST addresses the "how" of security, while COBIT addresses the "why" and "when."

Compliance: Not Just Rules, But Readiness

Here's the shift I want you to make: compliance isn't about fear—it's about readiness.

When you're compliant, you're not just avoiding fines. You're showing customers, partners, and regulators that you take your responsibilities seriously, that you're trustworthy.

Think about regulations like:

- **GDPR** and **CCPA** for data privacy
- **HIPAA** for healthcare
- **SOX** for financial transparency
- **FERPA** for education

They all demand the same thing: accountability. That's where frameworks like **ISO/IEC 27001** and **NIST** shine. They don't just help you check the box—they help you build systems that stand up to scrutiny and scale.

And when you layer in **CMMI**, you get a roadmap for process maturity. You move from reactive to proactive from compliance as a project to compliance as a mindset.

Integrating for Impact

You don't need a dozen disconnected systems. You need one integrated approach. Use the strengths of each framework:

- COBIT for strategic alignment
- ISO for structure and securityITIL for service management
- NIST for cyber resilience
- CMMI for process improvement

Together, they help you:

- Define roles and responsibilities
- Reduce redundancy
- Embed compliance into workflows
- Track what matters

And most importantly, they help your teams see compliance and governance not as extra work—but as how work gets done.

Culture is the Key

All the frameworks in the world won't save you if your culture resists them.

This is where leadership comes in. If you want governance and compliance to stick, you have to model the mindset:

- Be transparent about risks and tradeoffs
- Train your teams—not just once, but continuously
- Reward integrity and accountability
- Make audits learning tools, not landmines

Use ISO and CMMI's focus on training and continual improvement to build this into your org's muscle memory. Use NIST's Identify and Protect functions to keep risks visible and addressed.

When leaders walk the walk, teams follow. When compliance is part of everyday decisions—not a quarterly scramble—you win.

Case It Out

Let's say you're a healthcare leader managing HIPAA compliance. You use ITIL to build services with privacy embedded from the start. ISO ensures your information security policies are airtight. NIST helps you detect breaches faster. And CMMI keeps your processes evolving.

That's not just compliance. That's confidence.

Or maybe you're in finance, wrangling SOX. You integrate COBIT's governance model to track decision-making and ownership. You build real-time monitoring into your systems to catch anomalies early. You train your teams using ISO standards.

That's not just passing an audit. That's building trust.

What I Want You to Remember

Governance and compliance aren't about red tape. They're about results.

They help you:

- Align tech with business strategy
- Protect your organization
- Build systems that scale with confidence
- Create cultures of accountability and excellence

The frameworks are there. The playbooks are written. Your job is to lead the charge—to connect the dots between structure and strategy, between compliance and innovation.

Lead governance and compliance like you lead transformation: with clarity, courage, and purpose.

With purpose,

A Fellow Leader

Reflection Questions

1. Where in your organization is governance currently more of a formality than a force for clarity and alignment?
2. What would it look like to embed compliance into your team's daily workflow instead of treating it as a separate task?

Letter 7: On Making Tech Decisions That Move the Business

Dear Leader,

I know your calendar's packed, your inbox never sleeps, and every other day someone pitches a "game-changing" tool your business *has* to try.

Sound familiar?

Welcome to the modern leader's dilemma. You're expected to drive growth, scale with speed, and navigate a landscape where the tech stakes are higher than ever—and the BS is thicker than ever, too.

So here's the real question: how do you make smart, confident tech decisions without getting bogged down by buzzwords, vendor hype, or the fear of making the wrong call?

This letter is about that.

Whether you realize it or not, every tech decision is a leadership decision. The tools you greenlight shape how your teams work, how your customers experience your brand, and how fast (or slow) your company can evolve.

So let's talk about how to lead those decisions like the strategic driver you are—not a passive approver.

First, Ask: What Problem Are We Really Solving?

Before any conversation about features, pricing, or platforms, pause and ask: "What's the business pain here?"

Too many tech decisions start with solutions looking for a problem. Someone read an article. A team is frustrated. A vendor's demo looked slick.

But without a clearly defined business problem—and a clear desired outcome—you're gambling.

Instead, ask:

- What's broken or inefficient in our current process?
- How is this slowing us down or costing us money?
- What would success look like six months after implementation?

Get your team grounded in the problem. From there, the right solution gets much easier to spot.

Beware of the Feature Frenzy

Tech vendors are pros at dazzling you. AI dashboards, predictive analytics, automation bots—it all sounds impressive.

But don't confuse features with outcomes.

A tool can be loaded with bells and whistles and still do absolutely nothing for your core goals. That's why innovative leaders anchor every decision in **the relevance and simplicity of the use case.**

Ask:

- Do we actually need 80% of what this tool does?
- Can my team learn and adopt this quickly?
- Will this integrate cleanly with our existing systems?

If the answer is no, move on. You're not here to impress anyone—you're here to solve problems and drive value.

Involve the Right Voices Early

Want adoption? Want speed? Want fewer regrets?

Get input from the people who'll use the tool—before you buy it.

Too many tech rollouts fail because they were designed in a vacuum. The business didn't talk to IT. IT didn't talk to the end users. The vendor only spoke to leadership.

Break the pattern. Create a working group with cross-functional representatives—operations, technology, finance, legal, and customer service—who can provide input on what they need and identify potential risks.

Yes, it takes a bit longer upfront. However, you'll move faster after going live. And your teams will thank you for treating them like owners, not afterthoughts.

Run the ROI Equation—But Include Real Costs

Most leaders look at the sticker price of a new system. The smarter ones look at the **total cost of ownership.**

That includes:

- Implementation
- Training
- Integration with existing systems
- Ongoing support or licenses

- Productivity loss during the switch
- Headcount shifts or role changes

Only when you map all of those can you truly assess value.

But don't stop at cost. Look at potential value, too:

- Time saved
- Errors reduced
- Speed to insight or delivery
- Customer retention improvements
- Revenue lift from better data or workflows

Here's a simple **ROI Equation** to guide your thinking:

ROI (%) = [Net Profit / Total Cost Total Cost] × 100

Where:

- **Net Profit** = The total revenue generated by the investment minus all associated expenses (including the initial investment cost)
- **Total Cost** = All upfront, hidden, and recurring costs related to the tool

This forces clarity. It shows whether a tool earns its place—or eats your budget.

Know the Red Flags

Watch out for these warning signs before signing any contract:

- **No clear owner.** If no one's responsible for implementation and outcomes, it's a risk.
- **No integration roadmap.** If it doesn't play well with your current tools, run.
- **Training is an afterthought.** Adoption lives or dies here.
- **All hype, no metrics.** If a vendor can't show proven business results, walk away.

Pilot, Test, Iterate

Every tool looks good in the pitch deck. The real test is how it performs in your world.

Before you roll out anything enterprise-wide, **pilot it.**

Choose one business unit, one process, or one region. Measure success. Gather feedback. Refine the rollout plan.

Pilots protect your investment—and build confidence across your org.

Create a Post-Launch Plan

Your job isn't done when the tool goes live. The real work starts then.

Every tech decision should come with a 30/60/90 day plan:

- Are people using it?
- Are the right metrics being tracked?
- Are blockers getting escalated?
- Who's accountable for adoption and impact?

Treat every tool like a living system. Measure, tweak, and evolve.

Empower Your IT Team as Strategic Partners

Too often, tech decisions are made either entirely by IT without business insight or by business without IT insight. Both are broken models.

You need **co-ownership.**

Make sure your IT leaders are present at the strategic table—not just the implementation table. Ask for their input early.

Let them challenge assumptions. And make sure they understand the business impact you're aiming for.

IT leaders who feel ownership act like partners, not gatekeepers.

One Big Trap to Avoid: Shiny Object Syndrome

Just because it's trending doesn't mean it's transformative.

Don't chase AI, blockchain, or the latest martech tool just because everyone else is. Tech decisions shouldn't be based on fear of missing out—they should be based on **clarity of vision.**

Every decision should be evaluated by asking: Will this move our business forward in a meaningful way?

If not, save your budget. Save your time. Save your team's focus for something better.

What I Want You to Remember

You don't have to be a tech expert to make smart tech decisions. But you *do* have to:

- Stay grounded in problems, not promises
- Involve your people
- Ask better questions

- Demand simplicity and clarity

Because the tools you choose aren't just systems—they're signals. They signal what you value, how you think, and what kind of business you're building.

Lead tech decisions like a builder, not a buyer.

You'll go farther, faster—and with your team fully on board.

With purpose,

A fellow leader

Reflection Questions

1. What are the last three tech investments your organization made—were they driven by clear problems or shiny promises?
2. How can you strengthen the way your team evaluates the actual cost and long-term value of new tools?

Letter 8: On Collaborating Across the Aisle

Dear Leader,

Here's a leadership truth that holds across industries: no breakthrough happens in a silo. Technology doesn't move the needle unless it's aligned with business. And strategy doesn't stick unless IT is in the room where it's built. That's why collaboration between IT and business units isn't a luxury—it's leadership table stakes.

We've covered governance. We've explored alignment. Now it's time to focus on the human layer that makes it all work: the collaboration that drives transparency, speed, and trust across departments.

Let's talk about how to integrate IT into decision-making, choose tools that effectively connect teams, and build a shared language that breaks down silos.

Bring IT to the Table

The best decisions in any organization come from perspective-rich conversations. That means IT leaders cannot be on the sidelines of strategy.

They must be in the room—early, often, and with a clear mandate to advise, not just execute. Embedding IT in executive meetings, strategic planning sessions, and cross-functional reviews isn't just best practice—it's how alignment becomes real. When tech leaders understand the business agenda, they can anticipate needs, manage risk, and propose scalable, sustainable solutions. COBIT provides a governance framework to formalize this. ITIL gives you the language and tools to bring value to those conversations.

Want to go faster? Try adopting agile decision cycles. Small, cross-functional teams. Quick sprints. Iteration over perfection. When IT and business leaders work shoulder to shoulder in cycles, not silos, great things happen. You launch smarter. Pivot faster. Fail smaller. Win bigger.

Tools That Connect, Not Complicate

There's no shortage of collaboration tools out there. The trick is choosing the ones that do more than check boxes. You want tools that:

- Make updates visible across teams
- Centralize communication and planning
- Integrate with your core systems

Think platforms like Microsoft Teams, Asana, or Jira. Think dashboards that everyone can read—like Power BI or Tableau. Consider integrations that reduce friction, rather than just sending more notifications.

However, tools alone won't change culture—training is essential. Governance matters. You need champions who know how to use the tools and can teach others. You need systems that reward collaboration, not just individual output.

If your teams aren't using the tools, don't blame the tools. Dig into the why. Sometimes, it's training. Sometimes, it's redundancy. Sometimes, it's a trust issue. Your job as a leader is to diagnose and remove the blockers.

Speak the Same Language

Here's where most collaboration dies: miscommunication. Business teams talk revenue, retention, and ROI. IT teams talk platforms, patch cycles, and service requests.

You've got to build a shared language.

- Use analogies. Tell stories. Translate tech into business outcomes.
- Offer cross-training—finance basics for IT, infrastructure 101 for business teams.

- Create FAQ glossaries or shared knowledge bases in your collaboration tools.

One of the simplest, most powerful moves? Monthly cross-functional reviews where teams present *together* on shared projects. Not IT to business. Not business to IT. Together. It changes the dynamic from service-provider to co-creator.

Measure What Matters

If you want collaboration to stick, you need to show that it works. That means defining metrics that reflect *shared* success:

- Project delivery times
- Customer satisfaction
- Innovation output (new products, processes, or services)
- Cost savings from process alignment
- Employee engagement across departments

You can also measure the collaboration itself. Use pulse surveys. Run after-action reviews. Track tool usage—not just clicks, but conversations, files shared, goals hit.

And here's the key: act on the feedback. If your teams take the time to reflect, take the time to respond.

Leadership Sets the Tone

Cross-functional collaboration isn't a grassroots effort. It has to be modeled and reinforced from the top.

Here's how:

- Celebrate wins that come from cross-department effort
- Set joint KPIs—not just for delivery, but for working well together
- Include collaboration goals in performance reviews
- Hold regular leadership syncs that include both IT and business heads

Culture follows behavior. So show your teams what good looks like.

Real-World Alignment

Let's say you're launching a new analytics platform. Don't just have IT build it; marketing should also use it. Have them design it *together*. Let marketing define the KPIs, IT design the architecture, and both test the early iterations.

Or maybe you're optimizing a customer support workflow. Instead of IT creating a ticket system in isolation, bring in service reps. Map the process end-to-end. Let real users shape the solution.

That's how you avoid shelfware. That's how you drive adoption. That's how you unlock value.

What I Want You to Remember

IT-business collaboration is the bridge between strategy and execution.

Done right, it helps you:

- Align tech investments with tangible business outcomes
- Move faster and smarter
- Innovate from the inside out
- Build systems people trust and use

Frameworks like COBIT and ITIL give you structure. Tools provide you with reach. But culture and leadership give you traction.

Collaboration isn't just a skill. It's a mindset. A muscle. A habit.

Lead it like you mean it.

With clarity and confidence,

A Fellow Leader

Reflection Questions

1. Where in your organization do silos still exist between IT and business units, and what is one step you can take this quarter to break them down?
2. How well do your current collaboration tools and processes support cross-functional alignment, and what feedback have you gathered to improve them?

Letter 9: On Leading What Comes Next

Dear Leader,

You already know this: the pace of change isn't slowing. It's accelerating. What worked last year may not work next quarter. And as much as we talk about digital transformation, the real transformation lies in how you think, lead, and prepare your organization for what's coming next.

This letter is about looking forward—sharpening your lens on the future of IT and stepping into a role where you don't just react to change. You lead it.

Let's unpack the forces that are reshaping IT: industry convergence, hyper-automation, AI-era cybersecurity, and the rise of interconnected ecosystems. Then we'll talk about what that means for your strategy, your people, and your leadership.

IT Is No Longer a Department. It's the Business.

We've moved past the question of whether IT should be part of business strategy.

It *is* the strategy. The lines between sectors are blurring. Banks are building health apps. Retailers are becoming data companies. Manufacturers are launching SaaS tools.

This is industry convergence. And it means your IT function needs to be built for flexibility, speed, and cross-sector innovation.

Take healthcare. IT is powering everything from telemedicine platforms to AI-driven diagnostics. In the financial services industry, cloud-native tools are enabling real-time fraud detection. Across cities, public and private entities are collaborating on smart infrastructure utilizing IoT and AI.

What's driving all this? Integrated platforms, open APIs, and data-sharing agreements. If your tech stack isn't built to connect across silos—or industries—you're already behind.

Hyper-Automation Isn't Coming. It's Here.

We've all seen automation streamline tasks. But hyper-automation is the full-court press. It weaves together AI, robotic process automation (RPA), machine learning, and legacy systems to automate *everything* that can be.

Think beyond efficiency. Think accuracy, scale, and real-time responsiveness. In a supply chain, hyper-automation doesn't just track inventory—it predicts disruptions, reroutes deliveries, and reconciles accounts automatically. In finance, it flags fraud *before* it happens.

But this shift isn't just technical. It's cultural. It means redesigning workflows, rethinking roles, and retooling talent. It means upskilling your teams and challenging your org chart.

IT governance frameworks, such as the ones I discussed in Letter 6, provide the structure to roll this out responsibly. But the real work? That's leadership. Building a culture where automation is seen not as a threat, but as an accelerator.

Security in the Age of AI

As AI becomes core to operations, it also becomes a target. Cybersecurity in this era isn't just about firewalls and patching. It's about trust.

AI systems introduce new risks: biased algorithms, adversarial attacks, and data poisoning. As we integrate AI into customer service, healthcare, and finance, the stakes get higher. One glitch isn't just inconvenient—it can be catastrophic.

That's where frameworks like zero-trust architecture, AI auditing, and continuous monitoring come in. But tools alone aren't enough. You need policies. You need ethics. And you need a workforce that understands both.

Cyber resilience refers to building systems that can withstand attacks and continue to function effectively. It means disaster recovery plans that include AI outages. And it means training—not just your engineers, but your entire organization—on how to spot, respond to, and prevent AI-driven threats.

Building IT Ecosystems That Can Flex

The era of walled-off systems is over. Today's IT leaders operate in ecosystems. Cloud platforms, third-party APIs, open-source tools, global teams. It's all connected. Or at least it *should* be.

Winning organizations treat IT like a living network, not a closed system. This means prioritizing interoperability, investing in cloud-native infrastructure, and collaborating across vendors, sectors, and borders.

You don't have to build everything in-house. You have to build something that *connects.*

Start with readiness. Is your architecture built to scale? Can your data flow across platforms? Are your teams trained in ecosystem thinking—not just internal delivery?

The future belongs to organizations that can plug in, spin up, and pivot—fast.

So What Does This Mean for You?

It means you stop waiting for the future to arrive. You shape it. Here's how:

1. Lead with Vision, Not Just Tactics
Emerging tech is exciting—but it's not the goal. Business outcomes are. Anchor your decisions in customer needs, employee experience, and long-term value. Use tech to amplify that.

2. Invest in Adaptability
Train for change. Build systems that can flex. Create roles that evolve. Make agility part of your org's DNA.

3. Build for Security and Trust
If people don't trust your systems, they won't use them. Bake in security from day one. Be transparent about AI. Lead with ethics, not just efficiency.

4. Collaborate Across Boundaries
No more silos. No more "IT versus business." Build cross-functional teams—co-own outcomes. Make tech everyone's business.

5. Measure What Matters
Track innovation velocity. Measure the ROI of automation—report on cyber resilience. Make sure your metrics reflect the future you're building—not just the past you're maintaining.

The Real Opportunity

This isn't just about keeping up. It's about stepping up. As a leader, you have the chance to turn IT into a driver of growth, trust, and transformation.

You can:

- Harness hyper-automation to reinvent workflows
- Build ecosystems that unlock new markets
- Lead secure, ethical AI adoption
- Create the conditions for cross-sector collaboration

And you can do it in a way that's human-centered, outcome-focused, and built to last.

What I Want You to Remember

The future of IT is not a technology conversation. It's a leadership one.

Yes, you need to be aware of the current trends, including AI, quantum computing, and decentralized systems. But what matters more is how you lead your people through them.

The next wave of transformation won't be powered by code alone. It'll be powered by courage. By vision. By leaders like you who know how to connect the dots, build the bridges, and shape what comes next.

So step forward. The future is already here. It's just waiting for your leadership.

With clarity and conviction,

A Fellow Leader

Reflection Questions

1. What emerging technology trend poses the greatest opportunity—or threat—for your organization, and how are you preparing your team to lead through it?
2. In what ways can you redesign your IT strategy to foster greater adaptability, trust, and cross-sector collaboration in the next 12 months?

Letter 10: On Making Strategy Stick

Dear Leader,

You've come a long way. You've explored how IT drives innovation, builds trust, and creates competitive advantage. But this final letter is about what happens *after* the strategy is written. After the vision is pitched. This is about execution—the messy, vital, often-overlooked part of leadership, where great strategies either soar or stall.

Let's get clear: developing a long-term IT strategy isn't just about picking the right tools or forecasting trends. It's about commitment. About adaptability. About turning your strategy into something that's not just understood, but lived—across your entire organization.

So how do you do that? How do you make strategy stick?

Strategy Is a Living, Breathing Thing

Too often, strategy gets treated like a finished product. Something you "roll out" and forget. But the best leaders treat strategy like a living framework.

One that evolves in tandem with the business. One that's revisited, refined, and recalibrated—not annually, but continually.

That's especially true in IT. Technology doesn't stand still. Neither can your strategy.

You're leading in a world shaped by AI, cloud computing, and rapid digital disruption. What's effective today might be outdated six months from now. Your job isn't just to build a strategy—it's to make the *muscle* to evolve it.

That means:

- Creating space for feedback and iteration
- Embedding flexibility into your governance
- Aligning IT strategy with financial planning, risk management, and operational goals

This isn't just about tech. It's about mindset. Strategy isn't a milestone. It's a motion.

Make Execution a Team Sport

A brilliant IT strategy is worthless if it remains in the boardroom. Execution starts by making it real for every team, every function, every frontline leader.

But here's the truth: a lot of execution efforts fail because they rely on a top-down push. What you need is cross-functional pull. You need alignment, ownership, and clarity across departments.

That starts with a roadmap:

- Clear milestones
- Defined roles and responsibilities
- Visible metrics that track progress

And then you need something less tangible but just as critical: belief.

People don't follow plans. They follow purpose. So paint the picture. Show teams how the strategy connects to what they care about—their goals, their impact, their growth.

Make the strategy theirs, not just yours.

Train for Execution, Not Just Technology

Execution isn't just about systems. It's about skills. One of the most significant gaps in IT strategy isn't in the architecture. It's in the adoption.

That's where training comes in.

If you're rolling out new platforms, processes, or protocols, you need to equip your people. Not just with how-tos, but with *why-tos*.

- Create learning paths tailored to different functions
- Build champions within teams who can coach others
- Offer real-time support—not just documentation

And don't stop at launch. Make learning continuous. Technology evolves. So should your people.

Lead the Culture, Not Just the Plan

The hardest part of execution? Culture.

You're asking people to change how they work, think, and communicate. That's not a tech problem. That's a leadership challenge.

So lead it:

- Model the behavior you want to see
- Reward collaboration and initiative
- Normalize feedback and iteration
- Celebrate small wins as much as big ones

And above all, ensure that your values are reflected in your strategy. If you want a culture of innovation, your plan should leave room for experimentation. If you value accountability, your roadmap should include transparent check-ins.

Culture doesn't follow strategy. It fuels it.

Measure What Matters (Then Adapt)

Execution without measurement is guesswork. But measurement without meaning is just noise.

So define what success looks like—*early.* Then track it, refine it, and let it shape your next move.

Your KPIs should reflect:

- Business outcomes (not just tech milestones)
- Customer impact
- Operational efficiency
- Employee engagement

Use those insights to evolve your strategy. This isn't about perfection. It's about progression.

Think of your strategy like software. You don't ship version 1.0 and call it done. You patch, improve, and iterate. The same goes for your IT roadmap.

Your Final Playbook: What to Keep in Focus

Here are the five anchors I want you to hold onto as you lead your strategy forward:

1. Align IT with Business Objectives
Your strategy should drive business value. Full stop. Every tech investment should connect back to a customer outcome, a revenue goal, or a strategic priority.

2. Embrace Continuous Improvement
Your strategy isn't fixed. Create regular touchpoints to assess what's working, what's not, and what's next. Build in the habit of refinement.

3. Invest in Scalable Technologies
Choose tools and systems that grow with you. Cloud-native platforms, modular architecture, and AI-enabled insights aren't just trends—they're table stakes.

4. Balance Governance and Agility
Utilize frameworks such as ITIL or COBIT to establish

guardrails. But stay nimble. Flexibility is what turns strategy into opportunity.

5. Foster Collaboration Between IT and Business Units
Break the silos and create solutions. Ensure IT isn't a separate function—it's a strategic partner throughout the organization.

What I Want You to Remember

The best strategy in the world won't matter if it never takes root.

So this isn't just about building the right plan. It's about creating the proper habits, the right culture, and the right systems to make that plan *live.*

You don't need a perfect blueprint. You need a team that knows how to build together, adapt together, and lead through the unknown.

Because in the end, strategy isn't what you *say.* It's what you *sustain.*

Here's to building it better—and making it last.

With respect and resolve,

A Fellow Leader

Reflection Questions

1. Where in your current organization does strategy tend to stall—and what can you do to turn that inertia into momentum?
2. How can you better equip your teams—not just with tools, but with purpose—to take ownership of strategy execution across departments?

Final Letter: To the Leader You Are

Dear Colleague,

If you're still reading, you're not here for inspiration. You're here for alignment.

By now, you've lived enough cycles of transformation to know that strategy doesn't fail in the boardroom—it breaks down in execution. You've seen frameworks come and go, leaders pivot and stall, and teams run fast without running smart. You know the stakes. You also know the gaps.

What we've covered in these letters isn't new to you. But it may be newly relevant. Because as the demands on IT leadership expand, so does the opportunity—for clarity, for impact, and for the kind of leadership that outlasts the hype cycles.

This Isn't About What You Know—It's About What You Do Next

You already know how to build a strategy. You've done it.

But the next horizon isn't about sharper PowerPoints or tighter timelines. It's about how well you embed strategic thinking into the day-to-day.

How consistently you connect vision with behavior.How willing are you to create space for people to do the real work of change?

You don't need more theory. You need tighter execution. And you know that's a leadership problem, not a bandwidth one.

So this final letter is a challenge—to stop treating strategy as an annual deliverable and start treating it as a daily discipline.

You Set the Standard. Whether You Mean To or Not.

By this point in your career, your influence is baked in. People watch how you show up. What you reward? What you tolerate.

So ask yourself:

- Are you modeling clarity or creating confusion?
- Are you reinforcing speed or rewarding rigor?
- Are you giving people tools—or excuses?

Every missed conversation, every fuzzy KPI, every unchallenged behavior compounds. The standard is set, whether you name it or not.

That's not pressure. That's an opportunity.

Strategy Is Culture in Action

You know better than most that culture isn't what you print on posters. It's what happens when no one's watching.

So, if your strategy doesn't live in the routines, the feedback loops, or the performance conversations, it won't last.

The best-planned strategies don't lead the best organizations. They're led by people who make those strategies visible, contextual, and real.

If you want innovation, create space for experimentation. If you want ownership, let go of control. If you wish to execute, get closer to the blockers—not just the budget.

The Real Work Is Never Done

You didn't get here by standing still. And you won't stay relevant by settling.

The most respected leaders I know aren't the ones with the answers. They're the ones who are still asking better questions:

- Where are we playing not to lose instead of playing to win?

- What friction are we normalizing?
- What patterns need to be broken—and who needs permission to break them?

That's how you future-proof leadership, not by predicting trends, but by sharpening awareness.

Parting Words for the Work Ahead

Let me leave you with this:

You've earned your seat. Now gain the silence that follows it—by choosing to listen harder, challenge smarter, and lead with more clarity than noise.

IT doesn't need louder voices. It needs steadier ones. Yours.

You don't need more credentials. You need to keep making the decisions that matter, even when they're messy, slow, or unpopular.

Strategy won't save you. But discipline might.

Thank you for reading. For wrestling with the complex parts. For being the kind of leader who doesn't just want a better roadmap—but wants to build a better road.

With grit and respect,
Your Peer

Tools for Action and Additional Reflection

Letter One: On Thinking Like a Leader

Tools for Action:

- Strategic Thinking Canvas
- Role Clarity Framework
- Decision Mapping Template

Reflection Exercises:

1. Identify a recent decision you made. What strategic priorities shaped it?
2. What assumptions do you need to challenge to lead more intentionally?

Letter Two: On Building the Bridge

Tools for Action:

- Alignment Gap Analysis Worksheet
- Business-IT Shared Outcomes Map

- Cross-Functional Partnership Charter

Reflection Exercises:

1. Where do IT and business strategies diverge in your organization?
2. What shared success metrics could realign priorities?

Letter Three: On Owning the Table

Tools for Action:

- Stakeholder Influence Grid
- Meeting Impact Blueprint
- Value Narrative Builder

Reflection Exercises:

1. How are you currently showing up in strategic conversations?
2. What's one shift you could make to demonstrate leadership over support?

Letter Four: On Making ITIL Work for Humans

Tools for Action:

- ITIL Practices Relevance Map
- Service Improvement Opportunity Matrix
- Human-Centered ITIL Workbook

Reflection Exercises:

1. Which ITIL practices have become more about process than purpose?
2. How could you humanize one service delivery experience this quarter?

Letter Five: On Leading Change (Without the Hype)

Tools for Action:

- Change Curve Team Diagnostic
- Communication Cadence Planner
- Resistance to Resilience Tracker

Reflection Exercises:

1. What unspoken concerns are slowing your current change effort?

2. Where are you communicating facts but not feelings?

Letter Six: On Showing the ROI

Tools for Action:

- Impact-Driven IT Budget Framework
- IT-Value Communication Toolkit
- Metrics That Matter Scorecard

Reflection Exercises:

1. What results are you delivering that the business isn't seeing?
2. How can you reframe a technical win in business language?

Letter Seven: On Building a Digital Culture

Tools for Action:

- Digital Literacy Maturity Map
- Culture Conversation Starter Deck
- Experimentation Safety Net Design

Reflection Exercises:

1. What behaviors signal digital maturity on your team?
2. How can you reduce fear around experimentation?

Letter Eight: On Collaborating Beyond IT

Tools for Action:

- Collaboration Health Check
- Shared Language Glossary Builder
- Integrated Decision-Making Canvas

Reflection Exercises:

1. What's one barrier to trust between IT and another function?
2. Where could a shared success metric improve collaboration?

Letter Nine: On Preparing for What's Next

Tools for Action:

- Tech Trend Radar (customized)

- Scenario Planning Template
- Innovation Readiness Assessment

Reflection Exercises:

1. What emerging technology are you underestimating?
2. How are you preparing your team to be future-ready?

Letter Ten: On Making Strategy Stick

Tools for Action:

- Strategy Execution Scorecard
- Continuous Improvement Loop Map
- Communication Cascade Toolkit

Reflection Exercises:

1. Where is your IT strategy misaligned with execution?
2. What's one small win you can use to build momentum?

Exercises

Letter One: On Thinking Like a Leader

1. Conduct a 360-degree self-assessment focused on strategic impact and share insights with a mentor.
2. Create a weekly leadership journal that tracks decisions and links them to broader business outcomes.

Letter Two: On Building the Bridge

1. Facilitate a joint business-IT goals alignment workshop with key stakeholders.
2. Map a recent project across both IT and business objectives to identify missed alignment opportunities.

Letter Three: On Owning the Table

1. Rehearse and deliver a 3-minute value pitch on how IT drives business outcomes.
2. Audit your calendar for strategic vs. tactical meetings and rebalance time spent.

Letter Four: On Making ITIL Work for Humans

1. Interview end users to understand their service experience pain points.
2. Redesign one ITIL process flow to include empathy checkpoints or user feedback loops.

Letter Five: On Leading Change (Without the Hype)

1. Map stakeholders on a change adoption curve and tailor messaging accordingly.
2. Create a "Change Journal" for teams to log feedback anonymously over the course of an initiative.

Letter Six: On Showing the ROI

1. Redesign a report or dashboard to reflect business KPIs, not just IT outputs.
2. Host a monthly IT-to-business storytelling session to share impact case studies.

Letter Seven: On Building a Digital Culture

1. Facilitate a "fail-forward" retrospective on a past project to surface learnings.
2. Launch a micro-learning series focused on emerging tech and digital collaboration.

Letter Eight: On Collaborating Beyond IT

1. Run a "Day in the Life" exchange with a non-IT team to foster empathy.
2. Co-develop a cross-functional scorecard with business partners.

Letter Nine: On Preparing for What's Next

1. Host a future trends "debate club" with your team to build awareness and curiosity.
2. Conduct a digital skills gap analysis to identify readiness for emerging roles.

Letter Ten: On Making Strategy Stick

1. Launch a strategy roadshow across departments to build shared ownership.
2. Design a monthly pulse survey to track progress, blockers, and sentiment on execution.

Acknowledgements

To the leaders who mentored me. You know who you are, and I would not have been where I am without your guidance.

www.ingramcontent.com/pod-product-compliance
Lightning Source LLC
LaVergne TN
LVHW022012200926
848481LV00007B/2355
9798349519390